CW01162291

HULLABALOO!

WALSALL

Edited by Allison Dowse

First published in Great Britain in 2003 by
YOUNG WRITERS
Remus House,
Coltsfoot Drive,
Peterborough, PE2 9JX
Telephone (01733) 890066

All Rights Reserved

Copyright Contributors 2003

HB ISBN 1 84460 194 3
SB ISBN 1 84460 195 1

FOREWORD

Young Writers was established in 1991 as a foundation for promoting the reading and writing of poetry amongst children and young adults. Today it continues this quest and proceeds to nurture and guide the writing talents of today's youth.

From this year's competition Young Writers is proud to present a showcase of the best poetic talent from across the UK. Each hand-picked poem has been carefully chosen from over 66,000 'Hullabaloo!' entries to be published in this, our eleventh primary school series.

This year in particular we have been wholeheartedly impressed with the quality of entries received. The thought, effort, imagination and hard work put into each poem impressed us all and once again the task of editing was a difficult but enjoyable experience.

We hope you are as pleased as we are with the final selection and that you and your family will continue to be entertained with *Hullabaloo! Walsall* for many years to come.

Contents

Birchills CE Primary School
Kieran Powell	1
Ifrah Akhtar	2
Balpreet Kaur Gill	3
Sonia Iqbal	4
Jordyn Harris	5
Amy Shelton	6

Brownhills West Primary School
Jade Wright	7
Luke O'Shea	8
Charlotte Drewett	9
Lucy Howard	10
Natalie Platt	11
Thomas Egerton	12
Laura Day	13
Oliver Sharma	14

Delves Junior School
Sarah Kay	15
Gurdeep Singh	16
Charlotte Pritchard	17
Sarah Darby	18
Josh Nicholls	19
Laura Bird	20
Oliver Jevons	21
Faye Cooper	22
Daniel Dines	23
Narinder Kaur	24
Rajan Patel	25
Lauren Keen	26
Lauren Gilbert	27
Lauren Hughes	28
Jade Hind	29
Ben Lycett	30
Kiran Johal	31

Alice Beaman	32
Sabrina Boparai	33
Jack Rosser	34
Amy Harrison	35
Amrit Kaur	36
Jack Phillips	37
Luke Tamilio	38
Elle Gleeson	39
Iszac Khan	40
Bodie Morris	41
Ellie Morgan	42
Sarah Metcalf	43

Green Rock Primary School

Chloe Edwards	44
Frankie Saunders	45
Craig Whitticase	46
Jordan Spragg	47
Christopher Broadhurst	48
Petrina Ellis	49
Jack Owen	50
Tammy Stonard	51
Stephen Baugh	52
Craig Astell	53
Jamie Stonard	54
Rebecca Dean	55
Katie Broadhurst	56
Louise McDonald	57
Scott Davis	58
Sarah Murphy	59

Lower Farm JMI School

Rebecca Wheeler	60
Amy Craddock	61
Demi Tonkinson	62
Liam Dawkins	63
William Mulligan	64
Jack Smith	65

Jake Barrett	66
Rebeca Claybrook	67
Daisy Sanders	68
Lorna Smith	69
Lydia Sui	70

Pelsall Village School

Chelsea Billiard	71
Tara Neary	72
Melissa Cheal	73
Tayla Feasby	74
Charlotte Hardiman	75
Johanna Badhams	76
Stephanie Moriarty	77
Kieran Bunn	78
Nathan Griffin	79
Samantha Leek	80
Abigail Monk	81
Jessica Henry	82
Dominic King	83
Jonathan Jellings	84

Rushall JMI School

Lauren Griffiths	85
Clare Wynn	86
Kieran Wright	87
Kieran Giles	88
Christina Coyne	89
Andrew Baker	90
Michael Byrne	91
Jarrad Campbell	92
Baljinder Kaur	93
Nathan Breakwell	94
Christopher Wilkes	95
Amelia Adcock	96
Daniel Birkett	97
Kalvinder Kaur	98
Roscoe Anthony James	100

Charlotte Dawes	102
Alexander Lewis	104
Jack Marshall	106
Nicole Quinn	108

St Thomas of Canterbury School

Alexandra Birch	109
Chad Masters	110
Daniella Hickinbottom	111
Matthew Horton	112
Adam Crook	113
Jason Taundry	114
Joe Birch	115
Jake Birch	116
Ryan Kirkpatrick	117
Melissa Gripton	118
Laura Morris	119
Lucy Beech	120
Katrina Masters	121

The Poems

NEW BOY!

Look at him showing off with his clothes,
He'd feel more comfortable with a red nose,
Those Adidas trainers, that Burberry shirt,
It would suit him more with a fairy skirt.

What a show-off, what a tease,
Look at those shabby, skinny knees
And look at that chubby short arm,
At least he'd be good to work on a farm.

When he comes over, I'm not gonna talk,
I'll pretend I'm an animal,
I'll squeak and I'll squawk

And when it's all over, everyone will like me,
Not you, not her, not Mr T.

I looked at the show-off, then I looked at my mother,
I looked at the show-off a bit closer,
Then I realised . . . it was my three-year-old brother!

Kieran Powell (11)
Birchills CE Primary School

LATE!

Got up this morning,
Bed twanged, 'Get back in here.'
'Can't,' I said. 'Late.'

Went to the kitchen
Fridge rattled, 'Open this door.'
'Can't,' I said. 'Late.'

Went outside
Cat purred, 'What about a stroke?'
'Can't,' I said. 'Late.'

Went to the toilet
Toilet flushed, 'What about the chain?'
'Can't,' I said. 'Late.'

Went for a walk
Dog barked, 'Scratch my back.'
'Can't,' I said. 'Late.'

Got into the car
Car revved, 'More petrol.'
'Can't,' I said. 'Late.'

Went to fetch the children
Children screamed, 'Park! Park!'
'Can't,' I said. 'Late.'

Went to work
Friend giggled, 'Come to the pub.'
'Can't,' I said. 'Late.'

Ifrah Akhtar (10)
Birchills CE Primary School

TEACHERS, TEACHERS, UH!

I've had enough of teachers,
'Homework in tomorrow,' they say,
'Yes Miss,' we say, groaning while we listen.
Sometimes I think they're witches in disguise,
'Come along children,' they say in their horrible witchy voices.
Could they be aliens from the planet Homework
Or from the planet Be Quiet?
They must be from the planet Silence
Because they're always saying, 'Silence!'
Or are they just a human with a mind for teaching?
I guess we'll never know.

Balpreet Kaur Gill (11)
Birchills CE Primary School

THE TEABAG

I am lying in a smelly dustbin
I used to suck the sugar in the lovely tea
And swirl about in the hot water
And make it lovely and brown
But now I am lying in a smelly dustbin.

Sonia Iqbal (11)
Birchills CE Primary School

SIX MONTHS TILL BIG SCHOOL!

I wonder what big school will be like?
I have only six months to go!
Will I be nervous? Will I be happy?
Will I want to be back in primary school
Or will I meet lots of new friends?
Will the teachers be nice?
So I wonder what big school will be like,
As I only have six months to go!
Just what will I feel on the first day of big school?
So I wonder what big school will be like?

Jordyn Harris (10)
Birchills CE Primary School

A Winter's Day

The snow has fallen
In the night,
The sun shines on it,
Silver-white,
As it melts in the lane,
I see it trickle down the drain,
The children play on the sleigh,
Make snowballs and snowmen all day,
When night-time comes,
It turns to ice,
The children think it's very nice,
The children skid and slide,
Then they turn to hide,
Children get their skateboard and glide.

Amy Shelton (10)
Birchills CE Primary School

FRIENDS

A is for Adam, who always says madam.
B is for Ben, who held a wren.
C is for Chad, who is always glad.
D is for Dan, who is a man.
E is for Ellie, who met a girl called Nelly.
F is for Fred and his favourite colour is red.
G is for Gill, who took a pill.
H is for Holly, who is always jolly.
I is for Ian, who met a boy called Liam.
J is for Jade, who digs with a spade.
K is for Katy, who met her matey.
L is for Liam, who met a man called Ian.
M is for Molly, who had a dog called Polly.
N is for Nelly, who has a special teddy.
O is for Ollie, who has a sister called Holly.
P is for Pat, who bought a big mat.
Q is for Queen, who is always mean.
R is for Rob, who broke a doorknob.
S is for Sharnie, who is always having a barney.
T is for Tim, who is a bit dim.
U is for Ursula, who is always cooler.
V is for Vonnie, who met a dog called Ronnie.
W is for Wallice, who has a brother called Collice.
X is for Xena, who gets meaner.
Y is for Yonnie, who has got a sister called Connie.
Z is for Zack, who has a pack.

Jade Wright (9)
Brownhills West Primary School

FRIENDS

F is for friends to play with at school.
R is for Richard, your friend.
I is for igloo that we make at Christmas.
E is for excitement of the things we do.
N is for Nicholas, we are best friends.
D is for David, my best pal.
S is for Sharnie, her nickname is Barney.

Luke O'Shea (9)
Brownhills West Primary School

POP STARS

My favourite pop group is Hear'say
There is Kym, you should not get in her way,
Noel is lead singer and has a deep voice,
With Danny you will not have a choice,
Suzanne is a little bit loud,
Myleene always has her head in the clouds,
If you put them together, you get a group wiggling,
Some of them are always giggling.
The make-up woman is always busy,
At the end of the day, she is always dizzy.

Charlotte Drewett (8)
Brownhills West Primary School

MY ROOM

My room is quite messy with lots of fluffy toys,
They're big and small and don't like boys.
Under my bed, where we hang out,
'Mom, can I have some of your food?' I shout.

So up she comes with my food,
She is just like a dog in a bad mood.
So here's a poem about my room,
I'll see you later, see you soon.

Lucy Howard (9)
Brownhills West Primary School

LIVING WORLD

The mountains are so high,
As I watch the flies go by.

When I hear the hens,
As they go in their pens,

Sometimes I get in a flutter,
But it doesn't really matter.

The trains go up,
As I drink out of a cup.

Natalie Platt (9)
Brownhills West Primary School

MY PETS

My pets, they jump from tree to tree
They fly like a flea
They climb the wall
They play ball
They try to cry
And to reply.

Thomas Egerton (8)
Brownhills West Primary School

HOBBIES

I like to go swimming in the sea,
I would like to be an athlete
And run like the wind.
If I was a lifeguard,
I would watch over the waves.
I would play with dolphins
And see the high caves.
I love to play football,
I have a trainer called Andy Mulligan.
I think I'm a brilliant football star
And I think I'm my own guiding star.

Laura Day (8)
Brownhills West Primary School

FRIENDS

A is for Adam, who can't stop repeating.
B is for Barney, who can't stop cheating.
C is for Carl, who goes bananas.
D is for David, who loves piranhas.
E is for Earl, who can't stop reading.
F is for Fred, who can't stop weeding.
G is for Gary, who likes snails.
H is for Hagrid, who gets slapped by tails.
I is for Ian, who smells like plants.
J is for Jack, who gets ants in his pants.
K is for Katie, who writes neat.
L is for Luke, who likes eating wheat.

Rest of the letters fell off the cliff, sorry.

Oliver Sharma (8)
Brownhills West Primary School

DOG HAIKU

Through the field he runs
Getting faster as he goes
Tail goes *swish, swish, swish!*

Sarah Kay (7)
Delves Junior School

A Dog Haiku

Dogs bark at people!
Dogs love to go for long walks,
Dogs make super pets.

Gurdeep Singh (7)
Delves Junior School

A Monkey Haiku

Monkeys screech *oo, oo*
Monkeys swing from tree to tree
Munching bananas.

Charlotte Pritchard (7)
Delves Junior School

Cows

Cows munching green grass
Grazing in the farmer's field
Thank you for your milk!

Sarah Darby (8)
Delves Junior School

A Monkey Haiku

Monkey gone crazy!
Monkey swinging side to side
Monkey climbing trees.

Josh Nicholls (8)
Delves Junior School

A Dog Haiku

Dogs have appetites
They like to eat juicy bones
My nan loves dogs lots!

Laura Bird (7)
Delves Junior School

DOLPHIN HAIKU

The dolphin is swift
He can jump extremely high
A dolphin will hunt.

Oliver Jevons (7)
Delves Junior School

CAT HAIKU

My cat is lazy,
She really likes to kill mice,
She likes to lie down.

Faye Cooper (7)
Delves Junior School

HAIKU

Cheetahs run swiftly
Chasing animals for food
She has cubs to feed.

Daniel Dines (7)
Delves Junior School

DOLPHIN HAIKU

Dolphin in the sea
It swims in the sea all day
Water all around.

Narinder Kaur (7)
Delves Junior School

DOLPHIN HAIKU

A dolphin eats fish
A dolphin makes me happy
And gives people rides.

Rajan Patel (7)
Delves Junior School

HAIKU

Dolphins are my friends
Dolphins do not hurt people
I love dolphins lots.

Lauren Keen (7)
Delves Junior School

BUTTERFLIES HAIKU

Butterflies are bright
The butterflies fly gently
In the warm sunshine.

Lauren Gilbert (7)
Delves Junior School

HAIKU

The dolphin swims free
She jumps out of the ocean
And she jumps back in.

Lauren Hughes (7)
Delves Junior School

HAIKU

The snake is scary
He hunts daytime and night-time
He slithers on rocks.

Jade Hind (8)
Delves Junior School

MY CAT HAIKU

My cat is lazy
He lies down asleep all day
He doesn't go out.

Ben Lycett (8)
Delves Junior School

HAIKU

It looks beautiful,
It is a bit like a bird,
It is a pony.

Kiran Johal (8)
Delves Junior School

THE SNAKE HAIKU

I picked up a snake
It slithered out of my hand
Then it curled right up.

Alice Beaman (7)
Delves Junior School

BEAR HAIKU

My bear is poorly
He likes to roar when he's sad
Sometimes he gets mad.

Sabrina Boparai (7)
Delves Junior School

UNICORN

It has a big horn
It has four stumpy big legs
It has four giant hooves.
It has a black nose
With a black and white body.

Jack Rosser (7)
Delves Junior School

THE PANTHER HAIKU

As dark as a cloud
It rushes around like mad
Its claws are point-sharp.

Amy Harrison (7)
Delves Junior School

KANGAROO HAIKU

It's a kangaroo
It's got a baby pocket
It is really brown.

Amrit Kaur (8)
Delves Junior School

ZEBRA HAIKU

It is black and white
It is like a humbug sweet
It is really kind.

Jack Phillips (8)
Delves Junior School

MOLE HAIKU

What lives in a hole
Normally has soft black skin
And has a big nose?

Luke Tamilio (8)
Delves Junior School

CATERPILLAR HAIKU

The caterpillar
He gets bigger and fatter
Because he eats leaves.

Elle Gleeson (7)
Delves Junior School

A Snake Haiku

Snakes have a forked tongue
Snakes are very dangerous
Snakes are venomous!

Iszac Khan (7)
Delves Junior School

PYTHON SNAKES HAIKU

Snakes are venomous
Snakes are fast, they can bite you
Snakes eat mice and rats.

Bodie Morris (8)
Delves Junior School

A Butterfly Haiku

Wings flap and flutter,
Fly butterfly in the sky,
Fly back down again!

Ellie Morgan (8)
Delves Junior School

A Rabbit Haiku

Rabbit hopping round,
Munches juicy carrots - yum!
Hops back underground.

Sarah Metcalf (8)
Delves Junior School

WIND, RAIN AND SUN

Rain, rain, rain
Falls like water splashing,
Splashing and dancing in all the puddles
The wind blows it in your face
Making you like a stiff ice cube

Out comes the sun
Dries up all the rain
Out pops the rainbow
And makes everyone feel so good

The sun went down
The wind started whistling
Blowing things off their hinges
All the people ran away
Up above all of us, we heard a sudden *bang*
Oh no, it looks like another *gale*.

Chloe Edwards (11)
Green Rock Primary School

FOG

The fog is in the air gliding high like a bird,
For that it makes no sound,
Fog sneaks up making no footsteps.
Are they far or close?
Its fingers are in your face, making it cold and pink.

People disappear into the distance,
It slithers through your skin making you dither.
When it lands onto your clothes,
Leaving a damp, cold piece of clothing,
Fingers of fog touching your face.

Fog hovers in the sky like a fly,
Its floating version floats across the sky,
Then drops and lands on sorts of objects,
Skates amongst the paths
Shooting past other people.

The fog is in the air, gliding high like a bird,
For that it makes no sound.
Fog sneaks up making no footsteps,
Are they far or close?
It whistles in your face, making it cold and pink.

Frankie Saunders (10)
Green Rock Primary School

THE FOG

Quiet as a barn owl,
Gliding through the air,
Falling over the earth.

Sneaking down the street
Like a cat,
Waiting to strike its prey.

Swallowing the street,
Figures of people grabbed
By ice fingers.

Getting in houses,
The grass is turning white,
Footballs are like ice balls.

Wrapping round posts,
Blocking out the sun,
But the sun fights back.

Craig Whitticase (10)
Green Rock Primary School

SNOWFLAKES

Watching out the window,
Snowflakes drop on the ground,
Getting deeper each time,
Making not one sound.

The morning after came,
Kids put on their hats,
Rushing out to play,
Wiping feet on mats.

Evening came,
Snowman to build,
With lots of snow,
Children's pockets were filled.

Children's cold feet,
Time to go,
Snowballing friends,
With the snow.

Jordan Spragg (10)
Green Rock Primary School

THE RAIN

Plop! Plop! Plop!
On the rooftop.
Splashing in the streams
All around.

Tap! Tap! Tap!
On the window sill.
Seeping through every gap,
Till the gap is full.

Splash! Splash! Splash!
Like little bombs exploding
On the ground,
Then they can't be found.

Splash! Crash! Bash!
The water slowly goes
Back up to the sky,
So they say goodbye.

Christopher Broadhurst (10)
Green Rock Primary School

THE GALE

Winds were howling,
Fences were blown by fearsome winds.
Winds were growling,
Trees on the ground.

Rain danced in the puddles,
Rain was drumming on the ground.
Rain rapped on the windows,
Rain threw itself to the ground.

Hail crashed on the ground,
Hail shot all around.
Hail bounced off the path,
Hail crashed off the cars.

The gate had smashed,
The tiles had crashed,
The trees fell down,
The gale started to calm down.

Petrina Ellis (11)
Green Rock Primary School

THE RAIN

The rain elegantly dances in the puddles,
The rain shoots from the sky,
The rain can fit through the tiniest hole
And you never know when it will come.

The rain is wet and cold,
It crumples off the floor,
It splashes off the walls and houses
And makes everything go damp.

Nobody is playing out,
It's freezing cold and wet
And even if they did play out,
They'd slip and slide all day.

The rain is forced to the ground,
It's wet and cold all day,
It follows me everywhere,
So fight it if you dare.

Jack Owen (10)
Green Rock Primary School

THE GALE

The wind was howling,
The wind was lashing.
The wind was prowling,
The wind was thrashing.

The rain was splashing,
The rain was drumming.
The rain was clashing,
More rain was coming.

The hail was clashing,
The hail was drumming.
The hail was lashing,
More hail was coming.

The thunder was banging,
The thunder was drumming.
The thunder was clanging,
More hail was coming.

The gate had smashed,
The trees were down.
The tiles had clashed,
Blowing around my town.

Tammy Stonard (11)
Green Rock Primary School

SPRING

Spring is here, softly falling,
Flying through the trees
And the flowers drift gently.
The hilltops stalling through the woods,
But spring has got to go
And summer says, 'Hello!'
Now the summer takes over.

Stephen Baugh (9)
Green Rock Primary School

GETTING READY FOR SCHOOL

And he's off!
Slouching out of bed,
As if he couldn't care less.
He yanks open his wardrobe
And grabs for his T-shirt,
But it's his dog.
Oh no, there's only one hour until the bus leaves,
Will he make it?
He slips on his T-shirt,
Now his trousers
And last but not least, it's his jumper!
Oh no, half an hour until the bus leaves,
Can he do it?
He's looking around for his shoes,
Can he find them? Will he?
No, no, yes! They're behind the television,
Now all he has to do is get his reading book
And he's searching - he can't find it,
He smacks his face hard - he's left it at school,
Now to just tie his laces and get his bag,
Can he make it in one minute?
No, no, yes! He has, what a brilliant effort,
Now he can get to school on time.

Craig Astell (9)
Green Rock Primary School

Frankie's Rap

Frankenstein is hairy,
Horrible and scary.
He has got screws in his neck,
He boogies at night;
Gives the people a fright,
Turns them into shivering wrecks.
His face is green
And he's so mean.
He's a big, strong, ugly man,
People scream and cry,
As he stomps by,
On his way to visit his gran.

Jamie Stonard (9)
Green Rock Primary School

THE SUN

See the sun up high,
Passing through our sky,
It seems the sun is moving around,
Casting shadows on the ground.

Rebecca Dean (10)
Green Rock Primary School

SCHOOLDAY HORROR

And she's off!
She's getting out of bed and zooming into the bathroom,
Having a wash and brushing her teeth,
She's in great form!
She's running back into the bedroom at such great speed!
She's flinging open the wardrobe door!
She's grabbing her T-shirt, her jumper and her trousers,
She's put them on back to front, but she doesn't seem to care.
She's running downstairs,
What is this?
She's nicking her brother's piece of toast right out of his hand
Before he can bite it.
Now she's got her bag ready
And she's out of the door,
She's walking up the road,
She has reached the school,
The gates are closed.
It's a training day,
What horror!
That's it, from school horror,
Back to the studio.

Katie Broadhurst (9)
Green Rock Primary School

SNOW

S ee snow falling from the sky,
N ow it's time to say goodbye,
O h, what a shame,
W ho is to blame?
   Spring

Louise McDonald (10)
Green Rock Primary School

The Sun

The sun blazed at the people
The sun shot its rays onto the window
Now we are happy as the sun is out
The sun blazed at the green grass
The sun shot its rays at the people's backs
The sun blazed on the big puddle
The water disappeared
The sun blazed onto the greenhouse
The sun shot onto my neck
And all the ice from winter melted.

Scott Davis (11)
Green Rock Primary School

THE STORM

The storm is freezing
Freezing like a snowman
People walking all round
Cars speeding
Shops are closed
Bins are falling
Everyone is in their house
People are eating
Screaming and crying
Babies asleep
People scared
The storm.

Sarah Murphy (10)
Green Rock Primary School

FEELINGS

Love can be funny,
Love can be grey,
Love can be nice
Like a hot summer's day.

Hate can be evil,
Hate can be bad,
Hate can be upsetting
And it makes you feel sad.

Happy can be jolly,
Happy can be fun,
Happy can be you
When you're playing in the sun.

Sad can be sour,
Sad can be dark,
Sad can be lonely
Like walking alone in the park.

Just one question from me . . .
How are you feeling today?

Rebecca Wheeler (8)
Lower Farm JMI School

FEET

I'm talking about feet

Sticky feet
Scary feet
Spotty feet

Feet in cold water
Feet in new shoes
Feet in golden sand
Feet in shallow pools

Feet for doing
Feet for running
Feet for walking
Feet for sliding

Feet on land
Feet on dogs
Feet on sand

I'm talking about feet.

Amy Craddock (9)
Lower Farm JMI School

TREES

Trees, trees
In the breeze
When I look up
I get shaky knees
I run home to eat my peas
To find out I've lost my keys
Green, green leaves
That match my tasty peas
Trees shaking in the breeze
Shaking, shaking, knees, knees.

Demi Tonkinson (11)
Lower Farm JMI School

HANDS

I'm talking about hands,
Smelly hands,
Sticky hands,
Skinny hands.

Hands in a boiling plane,
Hands in a soaked house,
Hands in a decorated museum,
Hands in the slimy attic.

Hands for helping,
Hands for hammering,
Hands for swinging,
Hands for shifting.

Hands on an icy box,
Hands on a smooth table,
Hands are hairy!

Liam Dawkins (8)
Lower Farm JMI School

Don't Eat Cheese Before Bed

One night I was in bed
And I had monsters in my head.
Monsters, creatures, aliens and UFOs,
A shiver went from my head to my toes.
Dr Hyde being very mean,
Frankenstein was chasing me and making me scream.
I ran down the dark, creepy corridor,
The monsters were getting closer, more and more.
'Heeeelllppp mmmeee!' I cried,
My parents came in and told me it was all in my mind.

The next night came
And all I could think of was chocolate, sweets and a candy cane.
I thought it was very strange,
With this massive change.
So now, before bed, I won't eat cheese,
Hopefully there will be no more dreams, please.

William Mulligan (11)
Lower Farm JMI School

HANDS

I'm talking about hands

Flat hands
Hot hands
Cold hands

Hands in a hot bed
Hands in a funky playhouse
Hands in a cold classroom
Hands in a hot bedroom

Hands for playing
Hands for writing
Hands for rubbing
Hands for lifting

Hands on the table
Hands in a wacky house
Hands are funny.

Jack Smith (9)
Lower Farm JMI School

I'M TALKING ABOUT HANDS

Sticky hands
Bony hands
Hairy hands

Hands in the sticky studio
Hands in the bumpy box
Hands in the spotty sink
Hands in the punching plane

Hands for climbing
Hands for writing
Hands for driving
Hands for shifting

Hands on the sticky OHP
Hands on the funny sink

Hands are a pest.

Jake Barrett (8)
Lower Farm JMI School

FAIRY LAND

Once I had a dream
Of a fairy, she was so keen
She was a bit mean
She ate lots of beans
She was a bit lean
She had a boyfriend called Dean
The fairy was mean to people!

Rebecca Claybrook (8)
Lower Farm JMI School

CRAZY DAISY

There once was a cow called Daisy,
She was funny but awfully lazy,
She loved to dance,
She loved to prance,
That's why she's so crazy!

One day crazy Daisy went shopping,
Away she went a-hopping,
She went in a shop,
But brought a funny mop,
So now she cannot stop mopping!

So now Daisy's become funny,
For a change, she's earning lots of money,
But this isn't a treat,
For her poor aching feet,
For they are always hopping like a bunny!

So now you've heard the tale about Daisy
And how she came to be crazy,
She's sitting at home,
Always talking on the phone,
So again, she's become very lazy!

Daisy Sanders (11)
Lower Farm JMI School

FEET

I'm talking about feet

Bony feet
Stiff feet
Thick feet
Feet in the smooth bed
Feet in the rigid sand
Feet in the new wacky warehouse
Feet in the slippery train track
Feet for dancing
Feet for swimming
Feet for sprinting
Feet for peddling
Feet for the rigid mat
Feet on the wet slide
Feet on the rough aeroplane
I'm talking about feet.

Lorna Smith (9)
Lower Farm JMI School

HOCKET

There was a man named Hocket
He went to the moon in his rocket
His ears went *clang*
His rocket went *bang*
And he found a pound in his pocket.

Lydia Sui (11)
Lower Farm JMI School

SMILE

Everybody has a smile
If only for a while
So please try to smile!

When you walk down the road
You always try to smile
That's everyone's secret code!

People like to be happy
That's why you should smile
I really hate it when you're snappy

I like it when you smile
Smile not for the camera
For the whole wide world.

Chelsea Billiard (9)
Pelsall Village School

WORLD WAR 3

If there's a war, it will be bad,
But if it doesn't happen, we'll surely be glad.
If it happens once again,
It shouldn't be with France or Spain.
If it carries on for very long,
I'm sure something's gone very wrong.

Tara Neary (9)
Pelsall Village School

My Black And White Cat

One day I brought a pet
I had to take it to the vet
I brought a cat and it didn't like bats
But it liked rats and liked chewing on it
The cat's name was Jess
But I called it Cress
It liked running up trees
But didn't like bees
It liked sitting on my lap
But didn't like wearing a cap.

Melissa Cheal (10)
Pelsall Village School

WHEN I WENT TO TURKEY

When I went to Turkey
We all felt very perky
We went to our hotel
And I met a girl called Danielle
But when we all went home
We all felt very alone.

Tayla Feasby (10)
Pelsall Village School

MY PET CAT

I had a cat called Tom
He let off a bomb
He sat on a mat
I gave him a pat
Then he went outside
Because he didn't like inside
He licked my lolly
When it's raining, he's under my brolly
When he's hungry, he always wants food
Then he goes off in an angry mood.

Charlotte Hardiman (9)
Pelsall Village School

HOMEWORK

Homework, homework you're a pest,
My best friend thinks you are the best,
She hates me when I say, 'Will you do my homework today?'

I say, 'But this bit's hard.'
Then she says, 'It's like eating pie.'
Then I start to cry.
You're not gonna die,
If you do your homework today.

Do your homework!

Johanna Badhams (10)
Pelsall Village School

IN MY DREAMS

Last night I dreamt about a butterfly,
Flying up in the sky.
It spread its beautiful wings
And dreamt about amazing things.

The butterfly then had a dream,
He dreamt he was on a football team.
The players were very kind,
But when the ball came flying,
He did sure start crying.

The butterfly woke up
And decided to get tough.
The birds all started crying,
They thought that he was lying.

When I got up,
I got dressed,
Went to school,
Where I acted all cool.

Stephanie Moriarty (10)
Pelsall Village School

THE POOR GHOST

If you see the poor ghost
Stand to have a chat
Or give him a slice of toast,
But don't give him a mat.

You can share your friends with him,
That's maybe not a good idea,
They might be dim
Or have a big fear.

You can teach him funny things,
You could have him as a pet
Or even teach him to fling
And keep him away from the vet.

Kieran Bunn (9)
Pelsall Village School

MANCHESTER UNITED

They are the best
Better than all the rest
They're up for a good test
The red devil is a pest

Beckham is a right good kicker
Ferdinand wears a sticker
Keane eats a lot of Snickers
Beckham needs a haircut with the clippers

It's Man Utd.

Nathan Griffin (9)
Pelsall Village School

WHY DO WE HAVE TEACHERS?

'Why do we have teachers, Dad?
They give you work and nasty adding,
They give you singing lessons which are boring.
But still, Dad, why do we have them?'

'You have teachers to learn,
Even though you want your yearn,
They need you so they don't get the sack,
Even though you do a lack of work.'

'Why do we have teachers, Dad?
They give you a hard time,
They give you the cane,
Then you start off in pain.'

'You have your teachers
So they have someone to whack,
Even though you already knew that.'

Samantha Leek (9)
Pelsall Village School

How Many Countries Does The World Need?

There are loads of countries, so I look at a map,
I wonder why they are a funny shape, there is . . .
Australia, Austria, Brazil, Canada, my feet tap,
My feet are tapping, looking at a map, so I can see more,
Denmark, Finland, Germany and Hungary, all of these look so small.

It is amazing what you can find out at school,
India, Jamaica, Malta and the Netherlands, one big and one small.
That is the end of the geography lesson, time to go home,
I'll have to do more research at home.

Abigail Monk (9)
Pelsall Village School

MOUSE UNDER THE FLOORBOARD

There's something squeaking under the floorboard,
It's giving me a fright,
While I lay in bed last night,
I think I saw a tail,
It was pink and rather pale,
It's coming out,
I can tell, no doubt,
My mum came to see
What was bothering me,
She said it must be a woodlouse,
Ah, it's my lost pet mouse.

Jessica Henry (9)
Pelsall Village School

MY SWIMMER

My swimmer is a fish,
It swims around in a dish,
If you touch its scales, they are rough,
If you look at it, you will think it's tough,
My fish swims all day,
Apart from it sleeps in May.

Don't feed my swimmer hay,
If you do, it won't do or say,
My swimmer is cold and wet,
Don't forget it's my own pet.

Dominic King (9)
Pelsall Village School

THE OAK TREE

Autumn branches standing out
The wind has blown the leaves down
The tree has no clothes on
It is bare

Winter branches heavy with snow
Icicles hanging down
The tree is cold under the snow
Jack Frost makes the tree shine

Spring comes with new leaves
Buds growing in the warmer weather
Nests being built by the birds
The birds sing again in spring

Summer has big green leaves
Eggs hatch and baby birds cry
The warm breeze makes the leaves rustle
The oak tree is sad
Autumn will come soon.

Jonathan Jellings (10)
Pelsall Village School

POP STARS

P op stars are my favourite hobby,
O ctopus have long tentacles,
P igs are muddy and disgusting

S herbet is really sour
T op of the Pops is my favourite show,
A melia is the best mate I've ever had,
R abbits are the best pets in the world,
S inging is my favourite hobby.

Lauren Griffiths (9)
Rushall JMI School

POETRY

F riends are nice
R achel eats rice
I ce is cold
E mily is bold
N icole is naughty
D aniel tells porkies
S ea is blue
H old hands cos I love you
I nk is black
P ostman carries a sack.

Clare Wynn (10)
Rushall JMI School

FEAR

Once I had a dream
I did not know what I had seen

Its head came from down below
I thought it said a soft hello

I said, 'Get out!'
But it hit me with its big long snout

I said, 'OK, stay,'
But it just flew away.

Kieran Wright (10)
Rushall JMI School

A Man With His Frying Pan

There was a man with is frying pan
He wanted a suntan
When he got too hot
He had a plot
To get un-hot
With his magic pot.

Kieran Giles (10)
Rushall JMI School

WHERE I BELONG

School is like a prison
Where darkness has risen
I'm trapped
And I cannot see the world
I have to escape
I have to go home
Where I belong
Where I belong
Please let me go home
Where I belong.

Christina Coyne (10)
Rushall JMI School

THE HUNGRY DOG

There was a dog,
That sat on a log,
In the middle of the fog.

He looked in the trees,
For lots of bees,
But all he could see,
Were lots of leaves.

He was getting thinner,
He wanted some dinner,
He didn't have none,
So soon he'll be gone.

He wants some pie
And if he doesn't get it,
Soon he will die.

Andrew Baker (10)
Rushall JMI School

TIGERS

T igers are fierce,
I gloos are cold inside,
G oldfish swim in water,
E ars you hear with,
R ing, ring, the phone is ringing,
S orry is a word naughty people say.

Michael Byrne (9)
Rushall JMI School

ABOUT FOOD

There is a cake that people hate
I have tasted it
And I could eat eight

There is a chocolate that I love
People like it
So I gave it up

There is a toffee
That tastes like coffee
I ate it all and people copied

There was a fish
That looked like a dish
I tasted it and I didn't like it
So I kicked it out of the dish.

Jarrad Campbell (9)
Rushall JMI School

POETRY

F riends spend
R achel drives me round the bend
I say hello to Liam's sister, Chloe, because she is my friend
E lephants are huge
N icole gets confused
D ad's the best
S ophie was my friend

Baljinder Kaur (10)
Rushall JMI School

FAMILY

Families come in different shapes and sizes
They always buy you nice surprises
They're always there to look after you
So I write to tell you how much
Your families love you
Bye for now, it's time for lunch.

Nathan Breakwell (9)
Rushall JMI School

ROLLER COASTERS

Chinese Dragon ride

I am a Chinese dragon
I turn, crank and turn again
I rush down, up
I go into a tunnel
I rush downwards
Then we start again

Storm Force 10 ride

I am an orange boat
I whoosh down a water slide
I sail around a grass range
I crank up and turn on a turntable
And slide backwards
And I crank up again
I turn and slide down a big slope
And then we start all over again.

Christopher Wilkes (10)
Rushall JMI School

FRIENDS

Andrew is a scaredy-cat,
he watches telly on the mat.

Lauren is my best friend,
she lends me money to spend.

Rachel is funny,
she has a toy bunny.

Thomas loves art,
because he is smart.

Miss Cashell moans,
Mr Evans groans.

Nathan is sick,
because he is thick.

Ashley is good,
he has a blue hood.

Amelia Adcock (10)
Rushall JMI School

THAT'S MAGIC!

If you can do some magic
You're really quite fantastic
Can you make things float
Or turn things into a goat?

It's really quite fantastic
That wands are made from plastic
It really would be tragic
If wands stopped making magic

But that's not gonna happen
Cos magic is our weapon.
That's magic.

Daniel Birkett (10)
Rushall JMI School

TEN LITTLE CHILDREN
(Based on 'Ten Little Children' by A A Milne)

Ten little children
Standing in a line,
One fell over a cliff
And then there were nine.

Nine little children
At the school gate,
Along came a roaring lion
And then there were eight.

Eight little children
Travelling to Devon,
One vanished in a puff of smoke
And then there were seven.

Seven little children
Were playing with some sticks,
One got poked in the eye
And then there were six.

Six little children
Went for a walk, they found a hive,
One got stung
And then there were five.

Five little children
Were playing in the house, the door
Was open and one ran out
And then there were four.

Four little children
Climbed up a tree,
One fell down
And then there were three.

Three little children
Met a big fat cow, the cow went moo,
One child was scared
And then there were two.

Two little children
Had a yummy bun,
One got poisoned
And then there was one.

One little child
Played in the sun,
He got burnt
And then there were none.

Kalvinder Kaur (8)
Rushall JMI School

TEN LITTLE CHILDREN
(Based on 'Ten Little Children' by A A Milne)

Ten little children
Standing in a line,
One fell over a cliff
And then there were nine.

Nine little children
At the school gate,
Along came a roaring lion
And then there were eight.

Eight little children
Travelling to Devon,
One vanished in a puff of smoke
And then there were seven.

Seven little children
Standing on some sticks,
One fell off
And then there were six.

Six little children
Waiting to dive,
One fell back
And then there were five.

Five little children
Standing by a door,
One fell through
And then there were four.

Four little children
Making a cup of tea,
One got burnt
And then there were three.

Three little children
Falling in goo,
One drowned
And then there were two.

Two little children
Visiting the sun,
One got burnt
Then there was one.

One little child
On his own he had fun,
He got stabbed
And then there were none.

Roscoe Anthony James (8)
Rushall JMI School

TEN LITTLE CHILDREN
(Based on 'Ten Little Children' by A A Milne)

Ten little children
Standing in a line,
One fell over a cliff
And then there were nine.

Nine little children
At the school gate,
Along came a roaring lion
And then there were eight.

Eight little children
Travelling to Devon,
One vanished in a puff of smoke
And then there were seven.

Seven little children
Went for a walk, they found some sticks,
One got poked in the eye
And then there were six.

Six little children
Found a beehive,
One got stung
And then there were five.

Five little children
Playing with a door,
One got their fingers trapped
And then there were four.

Four little children
Climbing a tree,
One fell off
And then there were three.

Three little children
Drank some shampoo,
One got ill
And then there were two.

Two little children
Were having no fun,
So one went home
And then there was one.

One little child
Sitting in the sun,
He got hot
And then there were none.

Charlotte Dawes (8)
Rushall JMI School

TEN LITTLE CHILDREN
(Based on 'Ten Little Children' by A A Milne)

Ten little children
Standing in a line,
One fell over a cliff
And then there were nine.

Nine little children
At the school gate,
Along came a roaring lion
And then there were eight.

Eight little children
Travelling to Devon,
One vanished in a puff of smoke
And then there were seven.

Seven little children
In the woods,
Down came some sticks
And then there were six.

Six little children
On an assault course
One took a dive
And then there were five.

Five little children
Going home,
One hit the door
And then there were four.

Four little children
Playing on a hill,
One broke their knee
And then there were three.

Three little children
At the North Pole,
One caught the flu
And then there were two.

Two little children
Going into space,
One hit the sun
And then there was one.

One little child
Playing in a band,
Down came a drum
Then there were none.

Alexander Lewis (8)
Rushall JMI School

TEN LITTLE CHILDREN
(Based on 'Ten Little Children' by A A Milne)

Ten little children
Standing in a line,
One fell over a cliff
And then there were nine.

Nine little children
At the school gate,
Along came a roaring lion
And then there were eight.

Eight little children
Travelling to Devon,
One vanished in a puff of smoke
And then there were seven.

Seven little children
Went flying with a phoenix,
One got burnt
And then there were six.

Six little children
Went for a drive,
They had a crash
And then there were five.

Five little children
Broke the law,
One got sent to prison
And then there were four.

Four little children
Swam in the sea,
One got washed away
And then there were three.

Three little children
Went to the loo,
One got stuck down the toilet
And then there were two.

Two little children
Went to the school,
One went missing
And then there was one.

One little child
Ate a bonbon,
But then he choked
And then there were none!

Jack Marshall (8)
Rushall JMI School

My Teddy Bear

My teddy bear sleeps with me at night,
My teddy bear needs a light.

My teddy bear loves me,
My teddy bear can really see.

My teddy bear doesn't like mice,
My teddy bear is really nice.

My teddy bear is kind,
My teddy bear has a good mind.

My teddy bear can be mean,
My teddy bear is really clean.

Nicole Quinn (10)
Rushall JMI School

MY DOG, BODIE

My dog, Bodie sometimes bites,
He usually finds it hard but might.
We usually have to tell Bodie no,
Even if he thinks it means so.

My dog, Bodie barks and barks,
Even if he thinks it's dark.
We still, however, have to tell Bodie no,
Even if he thinks it means so.

Alexandra Birch (10)
St Thomas of Canterbury School

I Want A Word With You Lot

'I want a word with you lot,'
Our strict teacher said.
Out came the butter, the knife and the bread,
'We hope the word sounds tasty,'
All of Year 6 said.
'A good word would be
Chips, chocolate or pie.
Garden peas is a word for which we'd all die.'

'Enough of this gossip
And combing your hair too!
You'll like all words when I'm through with you.
The word I'm thinking of
Is not one word but two!'

'Clean up!'

Chad Masters (10)
St Thomas of Canterbury School

WHAT DOES YOUR TEACHER GET UP TO?

I saw Mrs Crawford in the cloakroom,
Singing *boom, boom, boom, boom.*
I saw Mrs Munnerley all alone,
So she pretended to be on her mobile phone.
I saw Mrs McCormack looking at her Winnie the Pooh socks,
Tigger looked like he had chickenpox.
I saw Mrs Vincent looking at her new shoes,
As she was walking into the ladies' loos.
I saw Miss McLoclan stuffing her mouth with jelly babies,
As she was walking into the ladies.

Daniella Hickinbottom (11)
St Thomas of Canterbury School

WHAT A GOAL!

England are the best,
The fans are cheering,
But they are a guest,
Everyone is hearing,
Ten to me,
Nil to Ryan,
The ball has gone into the tree
And here comes Brian.
My name is Jack,
On my work I lack,
My best mate is Mac
And I am going to hack my
Pack!

Matthew Horton (11)
St Thomas of Canterbury School

I Want A Word With You Lot...

'I need a word with you lot, Year 6 . . .'
The new teacher said.
Out came the knife
And the fork and spoon.
'We hope the words are very, very tasty,'
Said the cheeky, rickety Year 6.
'We hope it's not broccoli, sprouts or beetroot,
(Or anything disgusting in the dish.)
A delicious word would be chocolate,
Sweets and biscuits
And beans on toast,
We would all die for.'

'Enough of this stupid nonsense!
I'm fed up, I'm through!
You'll eat all your words when Mr Mooney's finished with you.
The word that you are wondering about is . . .
It's hard for you, your mouth dries up
And you go blue, the word is . . .
Homework!'

Adam Crook (10)
St Thomas of Canterbury School

THE ISLAND

Captain Blackbeard is sailing his ship,
He puts his hands on his hip.
The skull and crossbones on the sail,
Move about in the midnight gale.
He sees an island with a tall castle,
The drawbridge is shut, it's a lot of hassle.
A crack in the ship fills it with water,
It starts to sink, time's getting shorter.
One of the sailors swims to the shore,
He climbs up to the castle door.

Jason Taundry (10)
St Thomas of Canterbury School

SCHOOL!

Some people don't like school
Others think it's great
Some think it's OK
But it's what most people hate!
The biggest problem of them all
Is the head teacher
If you're naughty, he will say,
'Go home, we don't need you!'
Most people hate the SATs
They're the worst of all
And when you're in Year 6
You do them in the hall
When the SATs are over
Year 6 go to senior school
If you don't listen and you get answers wrong
You will look a right fool.

Joe Birch (10)
St Thomas of Canterbury School

SHARK WORLD

One bad day some hungry sharks came
They jumped out of the water.
They had their meal and a penguin yelled,
'Those sharks have taken my daughter!'

The penguins said, 'We'll get revenge.'
'But how?' another said.
'We'll go to their den and take a knife,
We'll kill them while in bed!'

So that's just what the penguins did,
They swam to the bottom of the water.
They made another penguin distract the sharks,
But another shark then caught her!

They ate her up with only bones left,
It was worse than being lost at Stonehenge!
'So I guess, fellow penguins,' the old king said,
'We'll never get revenge!'

Jake Birch (10)
St Thomas of Canterbury School

I Want A Word With You Y5

'I want a word with you Y5,' Mr Mooney said.
Out came the bread,
The knife and the butter,
'We hope the words are delicious,
Chocolate pie or sausage,' Ryan sitting at the back of the room said.
'I hope it's cake,
I eat cake by the lake.'

'Right, the word is not one word but three words,
Which are,
You're having homework.'

Ryan Kirkpatrick (10)
St Thomas of Canterbury School

WHAT TEACHERS DO!

I wonder what teachers do,
When we've gone home?
Do they drink fizzy pop
And eat lots of sweets?
I bet they play chase
And have a game of tig.
They have loads of fun,
Until half-past eight.
Tonight I'll stay and watch them,
To see what they do.
When I got there it was fun,
They were playing tig
And having a race.
When they had finished,
They looked a mess.
Shirts hanging out,
Laces undone.
I can't wait until tomorrow night,
To see them do it again.

Melissa Gripton (11)
St Thomas of Canterbury School

The Supply Teacher!

As I wait in dread and fear,
The angry supply teacher
Draws near!

I'm in trouble!
There's nothing I can do,
The supply teacher bellows,
'I'm not finished with you!'

She screams and she shouts,
Till her face goes red,
'That's it!' she yells,
'You're off to the head!'

Oops!

Laura Morris (11)
St Thomas of Canterbury School

ME AND YOU

Me and you are always together,
Sitting at the desk,
Doing all the rest.
Me and you are chums,
When we are together.
Me and you are like sisters
When we're by one another.
Me and you are ourselves
When we're . . .
T
O
G
E
T
H
E
R.

Lucy Beech (10)
St Thomas of Canterbury School

SCHOOL DAYS

'Sit down class,' our teacher says,
'Including you, that silly lass.'
In this week there's 7 days,
Monday 1st, start of the week,
When all the teachers start to teach.
Next it's Tuesday, on the roll,
Remember your homework in *big* and *bold*.
Now it's Wednesday, half the week,
Now it's Thursday, almost there
And now it's Friday, hip hip hooray,
I can't wait until the end of the day.

Katrina Masters (11)
St Thomas of Canterbury School